Workbook

For

Outlive:

The Science and Art of Longevity

(A guide to Peter Attia MD's Book)

Charles K. Spears

Contents

Introduction

From the beginning of time, people have been curious about how they may increase their chances of living a full and healthy life for a very long period. Many people are always looking for new methods to lengthen their lifetime and put off the aging process, which is why the desire for longevity has always been an essential component of human culture and history. People are becoming more conscious of the significance of living healthy lives and taking care of their bodies, which has led to a revived interest in the science of longevity in recent years, as a result of the improvements that have been made in medical science and technology.

This workbook is intended to serve as a useful guide that gives individuals the information and resources they need to live a longer and healthier life. It is based on the most recent research that has been done on the subject of longevity and aging.

The biology of aging, the role of genetics and epigenetics, and the importance of lifestyle factors like diet, exercise, and stress management are some of the many subjects that are discussed in this workbook. It also covers a wide variety of other topics that are related to the concept of living a long life. It offers a detailed explanation of the science underpinning longevity and how it may be practically applied to our day-to-day lives.

The workbook also provides applicable advice and methods that may be used to integrate healthy routines into one's everyday activities. This contains instructions on how to maintain a healthy lifestyle via dietary changes, physical activity, and practices such as meditation and mindfulness. These methods are designed to assist people in developing a way of life that fosters increased longevity and contributes to improved health and well-being on a global scale.

The Science and Art of Longevity is a resource that is both hands-on and user-friendly, and it is aimed to assist people in living healthier and longer lives. It gives a complete review of the science underlying longevity, as well as practical tactics and tools for implementing healthy behaviors into one's daily routine. It also offers a comprehensive overview of the science behind longevity. This workbook provides a comprehensive approach to improving longer life and general well-being by placing a focus on the need for social support and community involvement. Individuals can take charge of their health and make real changes that will assist them in living a longer and healthier life if they make use of the information and skills that are offered in this workbook.

Chapter 1

Mainstream medicine

In recent decades, mainstream medicine has made significant strides toward better diagnosing, treating, and preventing a wide variety of ailments. Yet, there is one area in which it has been generally unsuccessful: combating the illnesses associated with aging, which account for the majority of deaths. Despite considerable expenditures in research and development, we have not yet discovered viable medicines for many of these disorders, such as Alzheimer's disease, cancer, and heart disease. In this article, we will explore why mainstream medicine has had such a hard time making headway against these illnesses, as well as what may be done to improve the current state of affairs.

The fact that illnesses associated with aging are both complicated and caused by several different factors is one of the primary reasons why conventional medicine has not been able to make significant headway against these conditions. In contrast to infectious illnesses, which are often brought on by a solitary pathogen, the disorders associated with aging are frequently brought on by a combination of factors and typically manifest themselves only over a period spanning years or even decades. To provide one example, heart disease is brought on by a confluence of variables, including genetic predisposition, unhealthy lifestyle choices (such as smoking), elevated blood pressure, and cholesterol, among others. Cancer may potentially have several causes, such as genetic abnormalities, environmental exposures, and lifestyle factors such as smoking and obesity.

A further difficulty lies in the fact that the illnesses associated with aging are often not fully understood on a cellular level. Despite enormous efforts in research, we still do not have a complete understanding of the cellular and molecular pathways that are the root cause of many disorders. Because of this, it is challenging to design targeted medicines that are capable of treating or preventing certain illnesses effectively.

The illnesses associated with aging tend to be more frequent in people who are older and who may have various chronic ailments in addition to having complicated medical requirements. Because of this, it might be difficult to perform clinical studies and create therapies that are beneficial for this group. Also, older people may be more prone to experiencing adverse reactions to the drugs and other treatments they get, which may reduce the efficiency of these types of treatments.

There are considerable regulatory and financial impediments that stand in the way of the development of remedies for the illnesses that are associated with aging. The existing drug development regulatory system focuses on treating individual illnesses rather than tackling the fundamental causes of aging. This is because treating specific diseases is the primary emphasis of the regulatory framework. This may make it challenging for researchers to acquire funding and support for studies that are focused on aging as a target for therapy.

In a similar vein, there are monetary obstacles in the way of the research and development of remedies for the illnesses associated with aging. Most of these illnesses are chronic ailments that need to be treated and managed continuously. Because of this, it is sometimes difficult for pharmaceutical companies to recover their initial investments and turn a profit on their products. As a direct consequence of this, a significant number of pharmaceutical firms have redirected their efforts away from the development of medicines for illnesses associated with aging.

Despite these obstacles, there are reasons to have hope for the future of study into the illnesses associated with becoming older. In recent years, there has been a rising acknowledgment of the relevance of aging as a target for therapy. This recognition has come about as a result of increased research into the subject. The National Institute on Aging, which is a division of the National Institutes of Health, has initiated a significant research project focusing on understanding the fundamental biology of aging and creating therapies to prolong healthy longevity.

There has been an increasing interest in the research and development of medications that target the fundamental biological processes that are associated with aging rather than individual illnesses. For instance, researchers are investigating the use of senolytic medicines, which can destroy senescent cells that grow with age and are a contributing factor in a variety of illnesses associated with aging. In a similar vein, there is a rising interest in the use of pharmaceuticals that target the mTOR pathway, which is an essential component in the control of cellular metabolism and the aging process.

In contrast to the development of new drugs, there is also a rising interest in treatments that may promote good aging such as changes in one's way of life. These therapies include engaging in regular physical activity, maintaining a nutritious diet, and practicing stress reduction strategies such as meditation and mindfulness. While it is possible that these therapies will not be able to cure or prevent all illnesses that are associated with aging, they may assist to increase general health and well-being in older persons.

The conventional medical establishment has not been able to make significant headway in the fight against the degenerative illnesses associated with aging, which account for the vast majority of deaths. These disorders are often difficult to comprehend on a molecular level due to their complexity, many contributing factors, and multifactorial nature. In addition to this, there are considerable regulatory and financial hurdles that stand in the way of the development of medicines for these disorders. However

Chapter 2

Proactive strategy for longevity

The mainstream medical system has achieved remarkable levels of success in resolving urgent health problems and developing effective therapies for a wide variety of illnesses. Yet, the paradigm that is now used in conventional medicine is insufficient when it comes to treating the disorders that are associated with aging and promoting a healthy lifespan. We need to adopt a personalized, proactive strategy that focuses on promoting healthy aging and preventing age-related diseases rather than waiting for individuals to develop chronic diseases and then reactively treating those conditions. Waiting for individuals to develop chronic diseases and then reactively treating those conditions is not an option.

The approach that is now used in mainstream medicine is reactive rather than proactive. In most cases, patients don't go to the doctor until after they've already begun to have symptoms or after they've been diagnosed with a chronic condition. When this occurs, the emphasis changes away from avoiding the illness in the first place and instead is placed on managing the symptoms and treating the condition. This strategy may be successful in some circumstances; nonetheless, it is not optimal for fostering healthy aging and avoiding disorders associated with advancing age.

We need to take a more individualized and preventative strategy if we are going to be successful in promoting healthy aging and warding off age-related disorders. This entails emphasizing personalized risk assessments and preventative tactics that are adapted to meet the specific requirements and conditions of each particular person. We should not wait for patients to have chronic illnesses before taking action to prevent such diseases from occurring in the first place; rather, we should identify risk factors and take action to prevent those diseases from emerging.

The determination and treatment of the underlying causes of age-related disorders is an essential component of the tailored and preventative strategy described here. Inflammation, oxidative stress, and cellular senescence are only a few of the basic underlying processes shared by a number of age-related disorders. We can possibly prevent or postpone the beginning of several illnesses that are associated with aging if we can discover and target the relevant pathways.

Promoting healthy lifestyle practices that are proven to promote healthy aging is another crucial aspect that should be prioritized. This involves engaging in regular physical exercise, developing good eating habits, learning strategies to reduce stress, and participating in meaningful social activities. By encouraging people to engage in these practices, we may assist individuals in maintaining optimum levels of physical and cognitive function as they age, and we can also possibly lower the likelihood of age-related disorders emerging in those individuals.

Genetic testing and individualized medical treatment each have a part to play in this proactive and individualized strategy. We may be able to design targeted therapies for age-related illnesses if we first identify genetic risk factors for those diseases and then customize those interventions to the specific genetic profile of each person. Those who have a high hereditary risk for heart disease, for instance, may benefit from more aggressive measures to decrease their cholesterol or blood pressure. These people are more likely to have a family history of heart disease.

Using technology to achieve better health outcomes is yet another essential component of this tailored and preventative strategy. Individuals may get real-time feedback on their current health state through wearable devices, smartphone applications, and other digital health tools. These technologies can also assist people in tracking their progress toward achieving their health objectives. This may assist people in maintaining their motivation and engagement in their health habits, which may lead to improvements in their results.

We need to reform our healthcare system so that it places a greater emphasis on disease prevention and good aging. This requires designing compensation models that reward healthy outcomes rather than simply procedures and pharmaceuticals, motivating practitioners to concentrate on prevention rather than just treating illness, and investing in research and development that focuses on prevention and healthy aging.

There is every cause to be enthusiastic about the promise of this individualized, preventative approach to healthy aging and disease prevention, even though it is still in its early phases. We are acquiring a better grasp of the fundamental processes of aging and age-related disorders as a result of the fast advancement of research in domains such as gerontology, genetics, and digital health. We can enhance health outcomes and lessen the burden of age-related illnesses on both people and society as a whole if we take a tailored, proactive approach to promote healthy aging.

We need to replace the antiquated structure of conventional medicine with a tailored and proactive approach for increasing lifespan. This requires identifying and resolving the underlying factors that contribute to age-related disorders, encouraging good lifestyle practices, making use of technology to enhance health outcomes, and reorienting our healthcare system to place a higher emphasis on prevention and healthy aging. We have the opportunity to improve health outcomes and promote healthy aging for everyone if we take action now, rather than waiting for people to acquire chronic conditions.

Chapter 3

How to think about long-term health

Maintaining one's health over the long term is one of the most important factors in leading a happy and full life. As we become older, it is more vital than ever to adopt a preventative stance toward our health to ensure that we continue to have the best possible physical and mental performance. This entails formulating an individualized strategy for leading a healthy lifestyle, one that takes into consideration our requirements and the environment in which we find ourselves. We are going to have a conversation about how to construct the optimal health plan for you as an individual and how to think about your long-term health.

When contemplating one's health over the long term, the following considerations are important:

When thinking about one's health over a long period, it is important to consider several different aspects, such as one's genetics, the environment, how one deals with stress, and one's social ties.

Genetics:

The study of genetics is an important component of long-term health. The results of genetic testing may give very helpful information on a person's likelihood of developing certain illnesses and disorders, such as coronary artery disease, diabetes, and some forms of cancer. Equipped with this knowledge, you will be able to collaborate with your healthcare physician to design an individualized strategy for avoiding or treating the disorders in question.

Routines of daily life:

When it comes to supporting long-term health, adopting healthy lifestyle behaviors, such as regular physical exercise, good eating habits, stress reduction strategies, and social interaction, are all essential components. You want to make it a point to be consistent with these activities and to include them in your regular routine as much as possible.

Activities requiring movement:

As you become older, it is especially vital to stay active to keep your physical and mental functions in the best possible shape. It has been shown that engaging in regular physical activity may enhance cardiovascular health, lower the chance of developing chronic illnesses, and boost cognitive performance. At the very least, you should try to devote at least one hundred and fifty minutes each week to activities of moderate intensity, such as brisk walking. In addition, strength training activities should be conducted at least twice per week to keep the muscle mass and bone density that has been maintained.

Good eating routines include:

In addition to engaging in physical activity, cultivating good eating habits is essential to long-term health promotion. You should make it a priority to eat a diet that is abundant in fruits, vegetables, whole grains, and sources of lean protein. You should also try to reduce the number of processed meals, sugary drinks, and saturated fats that you consume regularly. It is also necessary to drink enough water to keep both your physical and mental functions at their peak levels.

Environment:

While thinking about your health over the long run, you should also take into consideration your surroundings as well as your exposure to harmful poisons and pollutants. Environmental variables, such as air pollution and exposure to chemicals, have the potential to have a substantial influence on one's health throughout their lifetime. It is essential to take measures to reduce one's exposure to these poisons as much as possible, such as installing air filters in one's house, consuming organic foods, and avoiding being around people who are smoking.

Stress management:

The effective management of stress is another essential component of long-term wellness. The presence of chronic stress has been connected to several unfavorable effects on one's health, including an increased risk of heart disease and other persistent ailments. To assist in the management of stress and to enhance long-term health, you should make it a goal to cultivate good stress management skills, such as mindfulness meditation or yoga.

Social connections:

While formulating a strategy for your long-term health, you should also take into account the social ties and support networks that you have. Isolation from others and feelings of loneliness have been shown to be associated with adverse health consequences, such as an increased risk of cardiovascular disease and a reduction in cognitive function. Keeping solid social ties throughout time, whether via membership in social groups or participation in volunteer work, may be beneficial to one's health and well-being in the long run.

Creating an individualized strategy for one's health over the long term:

While formulating a strategy for one's health over the long term, it is critical to adopt a comprehensive approach that takes into account each of these aspects. Thus, you will need to devise an individualized strategy that takes into consideration not just your genetics but also your lifestyle, surroundings, methods of stress management, and social relationships.

Collaborating with a healthcare professional who specializes in preventive medicine is an efficient way to establish a tailored strategy for one's health over the long term. This technique is one of the most successful ways. A doctor who specializes in preventive medicine should be able to offer you an in-depth analysis of the dangers to your health and work with you to devise an individualized strategy for disease prevention and healthy aging.

To assist improve your long-term health, in addition to working with a healthcare practitioner, you may also find it helpful to make use of the tools and information that are available through digital health. Devices that may be worn, such as those that monitor fitness.

Chapter 4

Cholesterol test at your annual physical doesn't tell you enough.

Why your actual risk of dying from a heart attack cannot be accurately gauged by the cholesterol test performed at your yearly checkup.

A cholesterol test is likely one of the most common tests you get when you go to the doctor for your yearly checkup. Your chance of getting heart disease, and more specifically, your risk of having a heart attack, may often be accurately determined by looking at this test's findings, which are often used by medical experts. Although this test has the potential to provide you with some helpful information, it is not enough to give you an accurate picture of the likelihood that you will pass away from a heart attack. This is true for several different reasons, all of which may be found here.

The cholesterol test will only evaluate your total cholesterol level and your levels of high-density lipoprotein (HDL) and low-density lipoprotein (LDL) cholesterol. Even though these are essential indicators of your cardiovascular health, a thorough evaluation of your risk of heart disease cannot be obtained by just looking at them alone. Inflammation, high blood pressure, and diabetes are three examples of other risk factors that may contribute to heart disease but are not assessed by a cholesterol test. Cholesterol is only one of several risk factors.

Even if you have high levels of LDL cholesterol, this does not always imply that you are at a high risk of acquiring heart disease. Many factors go into determining someone's risk for developing heart disease. Since it may contribute to the accumulation of plaque in your arteries, which can lead to heart disease, LDL cholesterol is sometimes referred to as "bad" cholesterol. This is because heart disease can be caused by plaque buildup in the arteries. On the other hand, not all forms of LDL cholesterol are the same. There are several distinct subtypes of LDL particles, and some of these particles are more dangerous than others. For instance, smaller, dense LDL particles are more likely to contribute to the formation of plaque than bigger, fluffier particles. The cholesterol test, on the other hand, is unable to discriminate between the various sorts of particles.

Your cholesterol levels may change over time, and a single test may not accurately reflect your overall risk of developing heart disease. For instance, if you have just had a meal heavy in fat or if you are under a great deal of stress, your cholesterol levels may be higher than normal. In addition, variables such as heredity and the use of medicine might affect one's cholesterol levels; however, these factors might not be taken into consideration during a standard physical examination.

The cholesterol test does not take into consideration the specific variables that might lead to heart disease. If your family has a history of heart disease, for instance, you may be at a greater risk for developing the condition than someone else with the same cholesterol levels but who does not have such a history. In a similar vein, your risk of heart disease may be increased independently of the levels of cholesterol in your blood if you are a smoker or if you lead a sedentary lifestyle.

It is essential to keep in mind that the cholesterol test is not a diagnostic tool. While it may give you an idea of how likely it is that you will develop heart disease, it is unable to say with absolute certainty whether or not you will have a heart attack. In addition to genetics, your age, gender, and general state of health all play a part in determining the likelihood that you may develop cardiovascular conditions like heart disease or have a heart attack.

To determine how likely it is that you will pass away from a heart attack, what steps may you take? The most effective course of action is to collaborate with your healthcare physician on the creation of an all-encompassing strategy that takes into consideration the unique risk factors associated with your situation. This may need further testing, such as a stress test or a coronary calcium scan, which may offer a more accurate evaluation of the danger you face. It could also require making changes to your lifestyle, such as adopting a heart-healthy diet, maintaining a regular exercise routine, and giving up smoking, all of which can help lower your risk of developing cardiovascular disease.

A cholesterol test is a good tool for determining your risk of heart disease; but, it does not tell you enough about your chance of dying from a heart attack. Several variables may play a role in the development of heart disease; a thorough evaluation of your risk should take into consideration both your specific risk factors as well as other tests that can offer a more precise evaluation of your risk. You may establish a strategy to lower your risk of heart disease and improve your overall cardiovascular health by working with your healthcare professional.

Chapter 5

Exercise is the most potent pro-longevity

The significance of physical activity to one's health and well-being as a whole cannot be emphasized. Participating in regular physical exercise provides various health advantages, including lowering the chance of developing chronic illnesses, enhancing mood and cognitive function, and increasing the likelihood of living a longer life. In this article, we will discuss the reasons why physical activity is the most effective "medicine" for promoting longevity, as well as the steps that one may take to get started on their journey toward competing in the Centenarian Decathlon.

Body:

Benefits of exercise for longevity:

Exercising regularly is, according to the findings of a large number of studies, one of the most effective strategies to extend one's life. It has been shown that engaging in regular physical exercise lowers the chance of developing chronic illnesses such as coronary heart disease, stroke, and diabetes, all of which rank among the top five main causes of death globally. Exercise not only enhances the function of the cardiovascular system but also promotes healthy aging by lowering blood pressure, decreasing cholesterol levels, and enhancing blood circulation.

In addition to improving metabolic function, engaging in regular physical exercise boosts insulin sensitivity and lowers the chance of developing type 2 diabetes. It is particularly essential for people to engage in physical activity as they age because it helps them preserve their muscle mass and bone density, hence lowering their risk of osteoporosis, falls, and fractures.

Research has revealed that keeping active may also boost cognitive performance. Memory, attention, and executive function may all be improved via regular exercise, which also lowers the risk of neurodegenerative disorders like Alzheimer's and dementia.

Exercise has been shown to boost mood as well as decrease stress, all of which may lead to improved mental health and general well-being. In addition, engaging in regular physical exercise helps improve immunological function, which in turn reduces the likelihood of contracting infections and diseases and promotes a speedier recovery from sickness.

Training for the Centenarian Decathlon:

It is necessary to start preparing for the Centenarian Decathlon as soon as possible to reach the aim of maintaining a high level of physical and mental function well into one's 100s and beyond. This entails participating in a wide range of activities, both physically and mentally, that are designed to improve one's health and well-being as a whole.

Physical training:

It is essential to begin with fundamental physical exercise when one is beginning preparations for the "Centenarian Decathlon." This may involve adding more physical exercise into everyday routines, such as taking the stairs instead of the elevator or going for a quick walk during lunch breaks. Other examples include climbing the stairs instead of the elevator. Building muscle and improving bone density are both crucial for general health and longevity. Resistance training, such as weightlifting or exercises using one's own bodyweight, may help to grow muscle and enhance bone density.

Aerobic exercise is equally important in the process of increasing lifespan. It is advised that people participate in at least 150 minutes of aerobic activity per week at a moderate level, or 75 minutes of exercise per week at a strong intensity. Activities such as jogging, cycling, swimming, and even brisk walking might fall into this category.

Balance and flexibility training are two more aspects of physical exercise that are very significant. Enhancing one's balance, flexibility, and coordination via the practice of exercises like yoga, tai chi, or Pilates may assist to lower the chance of falling and enhance one's overall physical function.

Cognitive training:

Training one's mind, in addition to one's body, is a crucial component in the process of extending one's lifespan. Studies have demonstrated that mental stimulation may aid to retain cognitive function and lower the risk of cognitive decline. [Citation needed] [Citation needed] [Citation needed] Reading, figuring out puzzles, learning a new language or instrument, participating in social activities, and other such pursuits may all count as forms of cognitive training.

Nutrition and lifestyle factors:

In addition to engaging in physical and mental exercise, elements related to diet and lifestyle also play a vital role in the promotion of longevity. Consuming a diet that is well-balanced and abundant in fruits, vegetables, whole grains, and lean sources of protein may help to lower the chance of developing chronic illnesses and may also improve general health. Moreover, avoiding harmful behaviors such as smoking and drinking too much alcohol, as well as obtaining sufficient amounts of sleep and managing stress, are all important contributors to good aging.

The role of technology:

Technology has been a key contributor to the progress made in the area of exercise and longevity research. Because of advances in wearable technology, people are now able to easily monitor their levels of physical activity, as well as their heart rates and patterns of sleep. These gadgets have the capability of providing useful feedback on one's progress and motivating folks to remain active and interested in their workout program.

Apps for fitness and internet tools are also available to assist users in tracking their progress and receiving tailored suggestions for exercises to do. Several of these sites make use of algorithms that are designed for machine learning to provide individualized feedback and suggestions based on the user's specific data.

The use of virtual reality technology in the enhancement of both physical and cognitive training is also becoming more common. According to several studies, conventional exercise and virtual reality exercise both have the potential to improve cardiovascular health and promote physical activity. The use of cognitive training in virtual reality may not only increase cognitive function but also lessen the likelihood of cognitive decline.

In recent years, telemedicine has also seen a rise in popularity. This field of practice enables patients to get medical treatment and guidance from a distance. This technology has the potential to be extremely helpful for those who have trouble accessing healthcare for various reasons, such as those who reside in remote locations or who have mobility challenges.

The most effective "medicine" for promoting lifespan is physical activity, which also has several positive effects on cognitive function and emotional well-being. Those who want to start preparing for the "Centenarian Decathlon" should participate in regular mental and physical exercise, have a good diet and lifestyle, and make use of technology to measure their progress and get individualized advice.

Individuals may increase their chances of living a long and healthy life by including physical activity and healthy behaviors as part of their regular routines.

Chapter 6

Forget about diets, and focus instead on nutritional biochemistry.

Here is why:

Diets have been the solution of choice for many years now for those who are trying to enhance their health and reduce weight at the same time. Nevertheless, the issue with diets is that they are often very restrictive and impossible to maintain, which may lead to emotions of deprivation and a sense of having failed. In recent years, there has been a trend toward concentrating on nutritional biochemistry and leveraging technology and data to customize eating habits. This change in emphasis has been accompanied by an increase in the use of personalized meal plans. This strategy is more efficient in terms of accomplishing long-term health objectives and is also less likely to lead to emotions of deprivation and failure on the part of the individual. In this article, we will discuss the reasons why you should forget about diets and instead concentrate on nutritional biochemistry, customizing your eating pattern with the help of technology and data.

Why Diets Don't Work:

The concept of calorie restriction, which refers to the practice of ingesting fewer calories than your body requires to lose weight, is a common foundation for many different types of diets. Unfortunately, this method is problematic because it does not take into account the complicated interactions that occur between nutrients and the biochemistry of our bodies. For instance, lowering one's fat consumption may result in a lower intake of necessary fatty acids, which can hurt brain function as well as the creation of hormones. Similarly, reducing or eliminating carbohydrate consumption might result in a lower intake of fiber, which is detrimental to the health of the digestive tract.

Diets are often unsustainable because they are extremely restrictive, which results in feelings of deprivation and, ultimately, leads individuals to return to their previous behaviors. Because of this, the vast majority of individuals who try to lose weight by going on diets end up regaining all of the weight that they shed, and in some instances even more.

The Benefits of Focusing on Nutritional Biochemistry:

The study of the intricate relationships that exist between the biochemistry of our bodies and the foods that we consume is known as nutritional biochemistry. Instead of taking a one-size-fits-all approach, we may customize our eating habits to meet our unique requirements if we pay attention to the biochemistry of nutrition. This allows us to avoid generic diet plans. To support muscle development and repair, for instance, some people may need more protein in their diets, while other individuals may require more carbs to fulfill their energy demands.

By concentrating on the biochemistry of nutrition, we can guarantee that our bodies are receiving all of the vital nutrients that are required to maintain a state of optimum health. Amino acids, vital fatty acids, vitamins, and minerals are all included in this category. It is possible for us to enhance the operation of our immune system, promote brain health, and minimize the chance of developing chronic illnesses such as heart disease, diabetes, and cancer if we consume a diet that is balanced and that is customized to our particular requirements.

The Role of Technology and Data:

Because of recent developments in technology and methods for analyzing data, it is now much simpler to tailor our eating habits to meet the specific requirements of each person. Wearable technology such as smartwatches and fitness trackers, for instance, can monitor our activity levels, heart rates, and patterns of sleep, all of which may assist us in determining the amount of energy we need. In addition, there are an increasing number of applications and online platforms that employ data analysis to deliver tailored nutrition recommendations based on parameters such as an individual's age, gender, weight, and level of exercise.

If we tailor our eating habits with the help of technology and data, we can be sure that we are satisfying our unique nutritional requirements and improving our overall health. In addition, if we keep a record of the foods we eat and keep track of how far we've come over time, we'll be able to make modifications as necessary and continue moving forward toward achieving our health objectives.

Since they are too restricted and fail to take into account each person's unique dietary requirements, diets are often unsuccessful and cannot be maintained for long periods. We can enhance our health, provide support for the biochemistry of our bodies, and achieve long-term success in achieving our health objectives if we instead concentrate on the nutritional biochemistry of food and make use of technology and data to tailor our eating habits. Hence, let's forget about diets and start concentrating on what counts, which is individualized nutrition that's based on each of our specific requirements.

Chapter 7

Ignoring one's emotional health while aiming for physical health and longevity may be a fatal mistake.

Since one's physical health and the length of one's life are often seen as the pinnacle indicators of a good existence, many individuals set their sights on achieving these as their primary objectives. To be sure, in the effort to maintain one's physical health, it is sometimes simple to ignore the significance of maintaining one's emotional health. We will discuss the significance of maintaining a healthy emotional state, as well as the possible drawbacks that may result from putting one's focus only on maintaining a healthy body and a long life.

The Importance of Emotional Health:

When we talk about our capacity to understand and control our emotions in a manner that is both healthy and productive, we refer to this as our emotional health. It is essential for one's well-being in general and also has the potential to have a substantial effect on one's physical health. Research has shown that emotionally healthy persons have a stronger immune system, are better able to deal with stress, and have a decreased chance of acquiring chronic illnesses including heart disease, diabetes, and cancer.

Emotional health is important for forming and maintaining fruitful connections with other people in one's life. When we are emotionally healthy, we are better able to express our emotions and wants effectively, which ultimately leads to connections with other people that are stronger and more meaningful. It also assists us in developing empathy and compassion for other people, both of which are crucial for establishing meaningful relationships and making a positive contribution to the communities in which we live.

The Negative Consequences of Neglecting Emotional Health:

When one is focused on maintaining their physical health and extending their lifespan, it is simple to forget about their emotional health. Yet, ignoring one's emotional well-being may have substantial negative impacts on one's physical as well as emotional health.

Chronic stress, for instance, has been linked to an increased risk of acquiring a variety of chronic conditions, including heart disease and diabetes. In addition, emotional health issues such as anxiety and depression that go untreated may have a substantial negative influence on a person's physical health as well. Research has indicated that those who suffer from mental health disorders have a shorter life expectancy in comparison to individuals who do not suffer from mental health conditions and have a greater chance of getting chronic illnesses.

When it comes to one's interactions with other people, neglecting one's emotional health may have a huge influence. When we are unable to successfully regulate our feelings, it may cause friction and tension in the interactions we have with other people. This may result in feelings of isolation and loneliness, both of which have the potential to have a detrimental effect on a person's mental health and overall well-being.

Strategies for Improving Emotional Health:

Enhancing one's emotional health is not only necessary for one's general well-being but also has the potential to have a major and beneficial effect on one's physical health. The following are some practices that may be used to improve emotional health:

1. Make a regular practice of mindfulness Making a regular practice of mindfulness involves being present in the present moment and monitoring one's thoughts and sensations without passing judgment on them. It can assist in the reduction of stress and anxiety as well as the improvement of emotional well-being.

2. Make connections with other people Developing constructive relationships with other people is a vital component of maintaining good mental health. Put forth the effort to interact with other people, whether it be by attending social events or

helping out in your local community as a volunteer.

3. Look for Help If you are having trouble managing your emotional health, you should look for assistance from an emotional health professional or a support group. They can provide direction and assistance to assist you in efficiently managing your emotions.

4. Engage in Self-Care It is important to your emotional health that you engage in self-care regularly. Find time in your schedule for things that please you, whether it's getting some exercise, reading a good book, or hanging out with the people you care about.

5. Develop an Attitude of Gratitude: Developing an attitude of thankfulness is an effective strategy to enhance one's emotional well-being. Set aside some time every day

to think about the things in your life for which you are thankful, whether it be your health, the people in your life, or the breathtaking scenery around you.

The state of one's emotional health is key to one's entire well-being and, may have a substantial influence on one's physical health. In the quest for physical health and longevity, it is possible to neglect one's emotional health, which may have substantial negative repercussions, including an increased chance of acquiring chronic illnesses as well as strained relationships with other people. We may enhance our emotional well-being and attain overall well-being and longevity if we regularly practice ways for enhancing emotional health. Some of these tactics include practicing mindfulness, connecting with others, seeking assistance, practicing self-care, and practicing gratitude.

Made in the USA
Las Vegas, NV
18 April 2023

70781856R00033